Snow Falling from a
Bamboo Leaf:
The Art of Haiku

Snow Falling from a
Bamboo Leaf:
The Art of Haiku

HIAG AKMAKJIAN

A *Noel Young Book*
CAPRA PRESS
1979

Library of Congress Cataloging in Publication Data

Akmakjian, Hiag.
Snow falling from a bamboo leaf: The Art of Haiku.

English and romanized Japanese.
Bibliography: p.
1. Haiku—Translation into English. 2. English
poetry—Translations from Japanese. 3. Haiku.
4. Haiku—History and criticism. I. Title.
PL782.E3A38   895.6'1'008   79-69
ISBN 0-88496-095-1

Acknowledgments

I am indebted to my nephew Adrian Akmajian, of
the Department of Linguistics of the University of
Arizona, for his reading of the manuscript and his
helpful comments. Of the texts consulted in the
preparation of these translations I would like to
express indebtedness to those listed in the Bibliog-
raphy.

CAPRA PRESS
P.O. Box 2068
Santa Barbara, California 93120

For Noel Young

It loved to happen.
Marcus Aurelius

CONTENTS

Part I

The Haiku Poem as Form

1

How the Haiku Form Developed

Many consider haiku to be literature's most subtle art form. It communicates emotion so seemingly effortlessly yet with such sophisticated force that Western prosody by comparison appears wooden and verbose, appears almost to be prose. Although the haiku form has been evolving for nearly a thousand years, its first impact on the West came only in the early part of the twentieth century, when the Imagists, a group of poets loosely and fleetingly united under the spiritual leadership of Ezra Pound, impressed by the brevity of the form, wrote poems they thought were in the haiku form. But were not: deceived by a leanness and frugality of language, they mistakenly believed that haiku were merely arresting images that give pleasure—pictures, not experiences. The quality they thought they saw in haiku could be described by Marianne Moore's comment on her own poetry: "I think the most difficult thing for me is to be satisfactorily lucid, yet have enough implication in it to suit myself." There is "enough implication" in haiku, but the correct use of the form goes far beyond. The Imagists never caught on to what that was—but, as we shall see, William Carlos Williams did, though he never wrote haiku.

That any first encounter with haiku should fall short of complete understanding is not surprising. Its form is unusual, similar to nothing in European art. No other poetic form is so concise: seventeen syllables in three lines, 5–7–5—and no meter. And a simple vocabulary: everyday speech.

But—and this was the point the Imagists missed—an important characteristic of the haiku is that its three short lines break into two unequal parts. There is a pause, a caesura, at the end of either the first or the second line. The pause juxtaposes what precedes with what follows—sometimes to shock the reader into a new awareness of life, sometimes to create a mood (another kind of new awareness). It is as if a haiku says: "Notice first this element. Now: here is another element, and see how the two unexpectedly complement each other" (or are really the same thing, or through their juxtaposition lend significance to each other).

This characteristic of the haiku was the revolutionary refinement introduced in the seventeenth century by Matsuo Basho, whom the Japanese consider one of their greatest poets. Until Basho's time (1644–1694), haiku, which were then called *hokku,* tended toward light verse, usually offering amusing conceits. One of the more frequently cited haiku of this early kind is from a *renga* (linked verse):

The hem of the long skirt of mist
Is drizzling wet.

The lady of spring
Must have urinated
As she got up.*

The verse is mischievous, charming, and pleasantly erotic. That it should so often be cited by critics for artistic condemnation—as what haiku is *not*—attests to its universal appeal: it has beauty, but a beauty of an order inferior to that of true haiku. The criticism that usually accompanies the citation of the verse has validity: this older "haiku" remains surface and entertaining. In it is no discernible statement about life, it has no psychological depth. It resembles, in this respect, though only superficially, Pound's "In a Station of the Métro" (whose level and beauty, however, are superior):

The apparition   of these faces   in the crowd:
Petals   on a wet, black bough.

Basho's famous crow haiku was the turning point:

on the dead branch
a crow settles—
autumn evening

---

*In "Introduction," in Issa, *The Year of My Life,* trans. by Nobuyuki Yuasa, Berkeley and Los Angeles, University of California Press, 1960, p. 15.

There is a pause at the end of the second line: now we may expect the contrasting element—Basho called the device "internal comparison" (or "surprising comparison"). Contrasted with a urinating lady of spring (a nonexistent being, however charming the image), a crow on a dead branch is real and has psychological overtones: more than just a picture of a crow on a bare tree as autumn evening descends, its "implication" is life itself in its aspect of isolation and loneliness. Nothing is contrived or witty, nothing clever or posed. And not a word of it is "poetic." On the contrary, haiku shuns the poetic and tries to sound spontaneous and thoroughly mundane. The best haiku have an impersonal tone while conveying a feeling about a small, freshly perceived truth.

Haiku originally were fragments of a longer poetic form called *waka,* which consisted of 31 syllables grouped 5–7–5–7–7. During the Heian period (794–1191) the *waka* was split into two independent sections, one of 17 syllables (5–7–5) and one of 14 syllables (7–7), each section linked to its neighbors by the association of words or ideas. In the Kamakura period that followed (1192–1392) the *renga* form was expanded from two parts to long chains, and from a double link to as many as 100 links. In expression of the Eastern philosophy of "selflessness," links were written by different authors working together. It was only from the fifteenth century on that the haiku began to be liberated from the constraints of the *renga* and recognized as an independent literary form.

It took the genius of Basho, another two hundred years later, to create from the modest 17 syllables of a haiku the masterpieces we associate with the form. Moreover, he promulgated an esthetics. A haiku has *shiori,* a "tender feeling," and *hosomi,* a "slenderness in its expression"— nothing excessive. It has *sabi,* "dry hardness." *Sabi* derives from *sabishi,* which means "lonely" or "solitary," a feeling Oriental artists and poets, who see human life as a small part of the universe, attach importance to. A haiku also has what Daisetz T. Suzuki called *wabi,* a taste for the quiet and homely: "*wabi* is to be satisfied with a little bit, a room of two or three *tatami* (mats) [a small room], like the log cabin of Thoreau, and with a dish of vegetables picked in the neighboring fields, and perhaps to be listening to the pattering of a gentle spring rainfall."

Aside from using everyday language, a haiku chooses for its subject the most common things and events of life. Although a *renga* might have as its subject "a green willow in the spring rain," that would be much too pretty, Basho said, for a haiku, which would prefer as subject "a crow picking mudsnails in a rice paddy."

To write a haiku the poet "gets inside an object, experiences the object's life and feels its feelings. You learn of the pine from the pine, of the bamboo from the bamboo": empathy—except that in the East, empathy is extended to things, not just sentient beings. A haiku poet gets inside a piece of wood, feels its "woodness." The poet "becomes" a flower, a tree, water. A haiku does not describe. Description introduces a division between poet and experience, stands outside them. In a haiku, poet and experience become one. All is related to all.

2

The Haiku Form and Feeling

A haiku achieves its effects through suggestion and nuance. Feelings, and especially feeling tones, are often expressible only obliquely. Eliot: ". . . the poet is occupied with frontiers beyond which words fail, though meanings still exist."

Basho was well aware of the sophisticated level of his poetics: "Anyone who creates three to five haiku in a lifetime is a haiku poet. Anyone who creates ten is a master."

But a haiku should not be written according to a poetics. Shiki (1867–1902), one of Japan's greatest haiku poets, wrote: "No process of reasoning should show on the surface." The writing should be laconic, with not one syllable more than necessary. (Ezra Pound: "Use no superfluous word, no adjective which does not reveal something.") Sentences are not required. The art is to make meaning clear through the least means—the "thrifty brush" technique, which in the West might bring to mind the compression of

Emily Dickinson sooner than the Imagists (Williams said of her poetry that it had a "distaste for lingering") or Louis Zukofsky's leanness and frugality (*hosomi*).

> Not the branches
> half in shadow
>
> But the length
> of each branch
>
> Half in shadow
>
> As if it had snowed
> on each upper half

The Japanese ideal of art is "the artless art": as effortless as snow falling from a bamboo leaf. A Zen master speaking of satori said, "If you want to see into it, see into it directly, because when you begin to think about it, it is altogether missed," and Basho would certainly have agreed with him.

To Westerners haiku is a curious form of poetry in that it shuns metaphor, simile, personification, and all the devices that we think of as almost synonymous with poetry. A haiku avoids adverbs and adjectives to the greatest possible extent. Even verbs, the backbone of language, are eliminated where they can be understood. Many haiku masterpieces have not a single verb, adverb, or adjective:

> Matsushima!
> Matsushima!
> oh! Matsushima!

Matsushima, an archipelago in northern Japan, is famous for its beauty, and Basho "describes" it by only naming the place and adding an exclamation of awe. It is a tour de force.*

Haiku are quiet celebrations of living. They express our deep kinship with nature. They imply a love of life that accepts its pain with no trace of bitterness, in fact knows that pain is an important part of being. Some haiku express a bittersweet response to life, and some a mood of revery—that state of mind that plays so small a part in Western sensibility. Some are appreciations of the beauty of existence, in agreement with Wallace Stevens: "There is nothing beautiful in life except life." A haiku is an insight into being. And because it is in the nature of insight to last only a moment, we understand the power of the haiku form: form and content are indissolubly fused.

A haiku makes you aware of life by intensifying perception. It is experience made vivid, a flash of awareness: Joyce's "epiphany," Melville's "shock of recognition," Stendhal's *"le petit fait vrai,"* Frost's "glad recognition," the Zennist's satori, and Conrad's "seeing" (the art of writing is "to make you hear, to make you feel—it is, before all, to make you see"). The "surprising comparison" is a leap that the mind makes. As Basho puts it—ever concretely—"the mind goes, and then it comes back again." The leap is the punch line of a joke, the sudden understanding accompanied by a laugh. Chuang Tzu said that true enlightenment comes as if you cannot contain yourself but must break into laughter

*See Appendix 1 for the romanized Japanese original and its transliteration.

before the story is finished. Epiphany, shock of recognition, satori—the terms are one: a sudden awareness of a truth about life. That is why haiku appeal so profoundly and so enduringly.

Almost all poets are in intimate touch with nature but perhaps none more so than haiku poets. Their love for whatever is natural and simple accounts almost entirely for their poetic impulse. Their close observation of the things of nature moves them to record the detail that "gives life to life." And the detail is often of the lowliest kind. They write about things and creatures that are not in themselves beautiful: the hair of a caterpillar blowing in the wind, a fly "wringing" its hands and feet. Compare the feeling between Buson's haiku of a butterfly sleeping on a temple bell (p. 87) and Shiki's of a firefly gleaming on a temple bell (p. 88).

Though the two haiku are markedly similar, how altogether different are the psychological responses they arouse. A slight alteration—and we perceive an entirely new bit of reality.

What is remarkable about these poems is that despite the modesty of their size and language they deal with the largest matters of all: life and death. An empty road as evening begins to fall suggests the transience of life and a peculiar forlornness we feel because we know in some inarticulable way that we are each profoundly alone in the world. As Suzuki put it, ". . . a certain sense of loneliness engendered by traveling leads one to reflect upon the meaning of life, for life is after all a traveling from one unknown to another unknown."*

---

*Daisetz T. Suzuki, Zen and Japanese Culture, New York, Bollingen Series LXIV, Pantheon Books, 1959, pp. 254–5.

And how economically Basho expresses nostalgia, that pleasurable pain of yearning for an earlier time. He says he longs to be in Kyo (Kyoto) even though he *is* in Kyo. His longing is not to traverse the distances of space but the untraversible distance of time.

Some haiku are an exuberant response to life. The little rain frog leaping up to land on a broad banana leaf, which sways and quivers under the impact of the jump, creates a picture that expresses a zest for living. There is nothing "meaningful" about a rain frog making an unpremeditated leap onto the broad surface of a banana leaf, yet as we see the frog sitting attentively on the leaf and swaying with it we feel something inexpressibly deep about existence.*

Equally impressive in haiku is the language: it is universally understood. Haiku are about toads, cuckoos, cicadas, fleas, snails, cats, and people. And they jump, fly, sing, crawl, sit, wonder. A haiku is never cerebral, which would be to write *about* life: a haiku *conveys* life. It never tells what the poet feels—the poet is not there: the *reader* feels. The haiku poet selects the true detail that evokes the emotion, which the poem communicates. Pithy and uncompromising, each haiku is life, the whole world.

In its love of the concrete, the art of haiku reveals another kinship, to Zen. Never is there abstraction in haiku—no reasoning, no intellection. The simple vocabulary makes its appeal to the senses, never to the mind alone.

---

*This haiku, by Kikaku (1661–1707), through a pun is in homage to Basho, with whom he studied: "Basho" means "banana tree."

Haiku stay close to the everyday sensual world. ("The Zen mind is the everyday mind.") They offer insight into things that are "useless"—such as feelings. A crow, with glistening black satin body, sits motionless on a cypress branch and broods over the snow, ignoring, across the clearing, the crested jay that jeers arrogantly. An icy snowfall pitters against the windows of the cabin in the woods, making the warmth of indoors all the more cozy. These are sights and sounds and sensations. They serve no purpose, move toward no goal, prove nothing. Yet they convey perhaps the deepest meanings that it is possible to experience about life. They evoke questions about existence that are so large that no philosophy can adequately frame them. They elude words and thought. They arouse a special feeling, the feeling that we are, for the moment, alive in some unusually vivid way. We become aware of *being in life* and enjoying being in life. All this happens instantaneously, in an intensification of feeling—life become conscious of life. Nourished by a rush of emotion, we feel incited to go on. Of how many events in life can that be said?

3

The Rationale of Selection

The haiku in this book have been selected because they are familiar to Westerners and because they make no allusions that require explanatory notes for their understanding. Why choose the familiar? Out of dissatisfaction with existing translations. The next chapter will discuss the problem of translation and elaborate the point.

To eliminate haiku whose allusions only Easterners understand is to eliminate haiku of great power and beauty. To the Japanese, Basho's Biwa haiku needs no elucidation. Biwa, near Kyoto, is a lake nestled among mountains and considered by the Japanese to be one of their great natural beauties. Many visit it each year to see the eight views it is famed for, one of them Mii-dera, a temple overlooking the water. Someone jokingly challenged Basho to put all eight views into a single haiku—an impossibility.* But Basho did the impossible:

seven of the views
were obscured by mist.
The eighth? I heard Mii-dera's bell

Another haiku requiring explanation to Westerners is Issa's "world of dew" haiku:

the world of dew is only a world of dew
and yet—
and yet—

The whole of Issa's life, which was a chronicle of heartbreak and misery, supplied the impetus for this haiku. Issa's mother died when he was two, and his father married a woman who, on the birth of her own child, relegated Issa to so much the stepchild status that when his father lay dying Issa wished he could die in his place. When Issa eventually married, his first and second child, sons, each lived about a month, and his third child, a girl, lived little more than a year. A fourth child lived a few months, and a fifth died less than two years old. Just before the fifth child's death, the mother died.

The "world of dew" haiku was written out of grief at the death of his first child. But grief is in conflict with his Buddhistic belief that death is a returning to the source, that like life, it is an illusion and no cause for sorrow. In fact, the entire universe is an illusion, a drop of dew—evanescent, soon to evaporate and be gone. Therefore it is wiser to love the things of this world in a nonattached way.

The poem affirms Issa's belief, but the very natural love he feels for his child sweeps aside philosophy and religion. His feelings are those of any parent. Stunned and in grief, what solace is any religious doctrine while mourning the death of one's child? This world may be only a drop of dew soon to vanish, but that is too abstract. The pain of grief, the pain of a love that is not so easily detached—that is real.

> the world of dew is only a world of dew
> and yet—
> and yet—

---

*For this and the next haiku, see Appendix 1 for the romanized Japanese original and its transliteration.

4

On Translating Haiku

Every good translator knows that language does not translate. Only meaning does. Yet there are very few good translations.

To translate without calamity the English "cold shoulder" or "crocodile tears" into a poem in another language requires art, not a dictionary. A good translation is a lens, transmitting light with minimal impedance. Like the viewer of a photograph, the reader never becomes aware of the apparatus that makes the seeing possible but only of the picture presented. The reader wants the poem, not the language of the poem, wants the feeling of the original, not lexicographic reverence—connotation, not etymology. An overpreoccupation with syntax and definitions can only get in the translator's way.

In translations, as in all writing, the reader's sensibility is what is appealed to. But the sensibility is peculiar to *the*

reader's own tongue, not the sensibility of the original language. To render Basho into English, the translator must respect not just the genius of the Japanese language but much more so the genius of the English language. It is in the music of English that Basho will communicate to us.

No one understood this better than Ezra Pound, who, according to Eliot, "invented Chinese poetry for our time." Pound did not go to the original Chinese characters or their Japanese equivalents but to the line-by-line English transliteration of the American Orientalist Ernest Fenollosa. A comparison of Fenollosa's draft with Pound's refashioning is revealing. He did not succumb to the usual fault of anxious faithfulness to the original, a devotion that is misplaced. Pound went so far as to drop two whole lines of Fenollosa's draft on the "general principle of not putting in mere words that occur in original when they contribute nothing to the *sense* of the translation." And he inserted words and lines of his own to achieve that sense. Pound includes in a translation the phrase "A wet leaf that clings to the threshold" even though "no wet leaf clings in the Chinese, and there is no indication that Pound supposed one did; he simply knew what his poem needed."*

Some translations of haiku use rhyme and assonance in a conscious attempt to avoid making the haiku a flat prose statement. But a good translation never fears that. It can't sound dull if it *is* a translation (a "carrying over") and not the rendering of equivalent words. Some haiku, like "Old pond: frog jump in—water sound," cannot be destroyed even in transliteration, so tightly constructed are they.

In my translations I have tried to stay as close as possible to the original ordering of words or images, departing from them, however, where to adhere too closely would violate either their sense or the sound of English. Just as the original haiku has to Japanese ears a natural flow, a translation into English should flow as naturally in English.

Robert Frost's definition of a sentence—"A sentence is a sound in itself on which other sounds called words may be strung"—is relevant to the problem of translation. Although a haiku is written primarily for the eye, like all good writing it is written by the ear. For this reason the most important part of a translation, assuming it conveys the full contents and intentions of the original, is the sound it makes in the mind. And the closer language approaches to the

---

*Hugh Kenner, *The Pound Era*, University of California Press, Berkeley and Los Angeles, 1971, p. 97.

vernacular (though not the colloquial), the more it is composed of sentence sounds. Many otherwise good translations suffer from the crippling defect of not having the natural rhythm of speech. Pound too was speaking of sentence sounds (before Frost coined the term) when he advised poets to put in a poem "nothing, *nothing,* that you couldn't in some circumstances, in the stress of some emotion, *actually* say." He exhorted his German translator not to "translate what I wrote, translate what I *meant* to write." "I'd like to see a 'rewrite' as if you didn't know the *words* of the original and were telling what happened."

My dissatisfaction with the existing translations of haiku led me to do that. The reader must judge whether the technique stands or falls in the attempts that follow. Many familiar haiku were chosen precisely so as to make comparison possible, as a test.

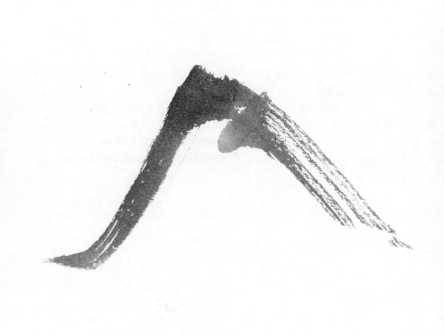

5

Haiku and English

With our brief understanding of the haiku form, what can we say about the writing of haiku in English? Can the rules of haiku writing be respected in a language other than Japanese?

To be able to answer these questions we must first list the elements that go into the making of a haiku. As we have said, a haiku expresses insight into life, and it does this economically, in approximately seventeen syllables. (The number seventeen is purely a convention and has no special significance.) The subjects of haiku are simple ones, usually common experiences. And haiku are concerned with human emotions, not actions: descriptions of nature and events used as a device for conveying feelings.

To the Japanese a highly important element is *kigo*, the season word. In each haiku a season is either described or implied. For example, "blossoms," which to the Japanese mind always connotes cherry blossoms, implies spring. In the East, the mention of deer means the autumn season just as clearly as mistletoe implies to many Westerners New Year's Eve. A careful observation of nature more often than not implies a season, whether intended or not. The mention of a crocus calls to mind late winter, a grape means early fall, and a moth, summer. The cuckoo usually means evening and often conveys a sense of poignancy: its call, which is usually heard at dusk, has to Japanese ears overtones of melancholy or nostalgia. They sometimes call the cuckoo "the bird of the other world." In Basho's famous haiku "cuckoo" has the sense of "the bird of time"—the past.

Feelings are only suggested, never directly expressed, to leave room for that peculiar sense of the unknown that we associate with the only deep mystery we know—life itself. "Life" can't be expressed: it is larger than any expression. But brief though haiku are, each one is an insight into some aspect of being. A haiku expresses an intimate kinship with ordinary things, a tree branch, a rock, pattering rainfall— homely details, most of which are visual or auditory, about which we have feelings that evoke a sense of our oneness with nature. Part of a haiku's power depends on the avoidance of generalizations. A haiku seldom deals with things in groups: not flowers but *a* flower—not morning glories, *a* morning glory. A haiku omits as many words as it can without losing meaning and plays on its few words so that the music of the language, aided by onomotapoeia, makes it, in the original, pleasurable to read aloud and hear.

Yet it is wise to bear in mind that a haiku makes no

attempt to be beautiful. Like all good writing, it aims primarily at meaning, and not through intellect but feeling. The impulse to write is a genuinely felt emotion that arises spontaneously. The parts of a haiku come to the writer the way insight does: *somehow.* Although revision is often necessary, there is no room for self-consciousness or artifice that shows. Because above all, a haiku sounds natural and effortless, as if anyone could have written it.

Clearly, then, haiku can be written in any language. The only element that might present a problem in some languages, of which English is preeminently one, is the seventeen-syllable arrangement. Although that convention is severely confining in English, it is possible to achieve— though entirely unnecessary. English words, so many of which have Latin origins, can be cumbersomely multisyllabic, and English syntax requires parts of speech that pile on still more syllables. A strict syllable count is the least important part of a haiku. Even the Japanese poets honor this rule more in the breach than in the keeping. Thousands of well-known Japanese haiku have between twelve and twenty-two syllables. According to Shiki, "Break rules if necessary."

What counts as most important in writing a haiku is the device of internal comparison, the juxtaposed detail that communicates insight, expressed through a "slenderness" of language.

Anyone who can write a brief poem embodying these principles, in whatever language, is a haiku poet. A supreme example of the art, though not intended as a haiku, is William Carlos Williams' poem

so much depends
upon

a red wheel
barrow

glazed with rain
water

beside the white
chickens

The first four words are what make it a haiku: "so much depends / upon." Note that without those introductory words the poem would be only an image, without much meaning—in the manner of the Imagists. But by including the first four words, the remainder of the poem is in significant juxtaposition to the sense of the opening two lines, the internal comparison that comes after the caesura. Played one against the other, they offer so profound an insight into existence that it is impossible to articulate the insight in any other way.

And how natural the language is. Yet it is not cut-up prose. In fact, the arrangement of words is a daring one because an alteration as seemingly trivial as merely changing the typography reduces the poem to a banal statement, completely empty of meaning:

So much depends upon a red wheel barrow glazed with rain water beside the white chickens.

"Wheel barrow" are the season words. We see the barrow sitting in the barnyard, left there by the farmer or gardener, who is perhaps off somewhere weeding the fenced-in plot of vegetables or transplanting some seedlings from pots to soil in late spring. His work momentarily completed, he left the wheel barrow wherever it happened to be, and it got rained on. Now that the rain has ended, the chickens are out wandering around as usual, clucking and pecking. Twenty-two syllables.

6

Technical Notes on Translating from the Japanese

Of the stylistic possibilities of English, I have cho-
sen, in the spirit of Basho's *hosomi* (slenderness of expres-
sion), the least means. For example, I have used the lower
case throughout except for place names and where a sen-
tence begins in the middle of a haiku. The purely formal
convention of capitalizing initial letters seems cumbersome
in a haiku. Since grammar and syntax are needed only for
sense, formal properties have been kept to the minimum.

Although I have not used titles, the practice of using
them—Henderson does, for example (see Bibliography, p.
112)—can be defended. Some of the best haiku occur in
travel diaries, their context in effect constituting a title.
Other haiku are accompanied by a headnote that makes the
point explicit. (One of Basho's headnotes reads, "I want to
cry out that I am lonely, but no one asks me how I feel.") But
to add on a title with each haiku in translation is like
supplying a fourth line to explain the meaning rather than

letting the seventeen or so syllables do the work.

The problems in translating haiku are many. One is the syllable count. It is unrewarding to attempt in English three lines of (approximately) 5–7–5, and even Basho's famous crow haiku, to cite only one of many examples, is written 5–9–5. English syntax is against a too strict adherence to this rule—English words are seldom the same length as their Japanese counterparts. Sentence sound and meaning, therefore, have been given preference.

In Japanese there are no words corresponding to "a," "an," and "the." Yet in English, articles are unavoidable and important: an ill-considered choice among them alters meaning especially but also mood and feeling.

Nouns do not take a special plural form in Japanese. The word *semi* ("cicada") means one or many cicadas, the number understood in context, just as we have no difficulty in English in understanding *deer* or *fish* to be singular or plural. In some contexts the number is vague, and perhaps intentionally, which accounts for some variations in translation. Pronouns are omitted, and neither nouns nor pronouns have cases. Verbs indicate only tense, not person or number, and they come at the end of the sentence. Japanese sentence order is subject-object-verb. Conjunctions come at the end of the clause they govern, and subordinate clauses generally come before the principal clause: in Japanese you cannot say "I would if I could" but must say "If I could, I would."

The relationship between words in a sentence is indicated by particles, which are postpositions. The most common are these:

ga   When it occurs in older haiku, *ga* usually indicates the possessive, and in modern haiku, indicates the subject of the verb. When it is used between phrases it can have the significance of "but."

ka   Indicates a question.

mo   After verbs, *mo* means "even though," "even if." After a noun it means that what has been named is to be added to something else. If that thing has already been mentioned, *mo* means "also." If it has not been mentioned, *mo* approximates "even."

ni   Means "at," "to," "in," "for," "by," "from," "through"—many of the prepositions of English. The word preceding *ni* is understood to be at rest. In Buson's line *tsurigane ni* ("on the temple bell") it is implied that the bell is not in motion.

no   A postposition usually meaning "of" and indicating possession or has adjectival meaning. *Nihon no ocha* means "Japan's tea," for which we would say, "Japanese tea." (The Japanese language has fewer adjectives than English.)

o   Follows the direct object.

to   Means "that" or "thus." In a series of nouns separated by *to* it means "and." It can also mean "if" or "when." For example, in Japanese: "That takes place, and after that . . ." In English we would express it thus: *"If* that happens, *then* . . ."

41

wa   Means "as for" and often indicates the subject of a clause. It can be used to suggest a comparison, and when spoken is usually followed by a pause.

wo .   Same as *o*. Postposition indicating that something is to be acted on.

yo   Means "exclamation point."

zo   An intensifier.

Apart from these particles there are *kireji*. *Kireji* words are words that "cut off." That is, they indicate a pause or a stop.

kana   Means "Ah!" or "Oh!" usually at the end of a haiku, in place of a verb.

keri   Having no special meaning now, it was originally a verb suffix indicating a past tense. It marks a pause or a stop.

ya   Usually has the meaning of a significant pause best translated as a colon or a dash (sometimes a period or an exclamation point). It divides a haiku into its two elements with the suggestion that they be contrasted.

yara   Means "I wonder!"

All particles and *kireji* affect the words that *precede* them.

To compensate for some of the drawbacks of translation, translating Japanese into English is greatly helped by

42

our punctuation and stylistic devices. Colons, dashes, and exclamation points, and more than that, the use of italics for emphasis, irony, or humor, contribute much to sense without adding words.

In the romanized Japanese accompanying the haiku that follow, the vowels are pronounced as in Italian and the consonants as in English.

NOTE: In the transliteration in romanized Japanese accompanying the original haiku [nom.] means "nominative," [acc.] "accusative," and [poss.] "possessive." In the Japanese, ō means that the vowel is lengthened.

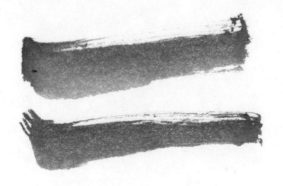

Part II

The Haiku

the old pond—
a frog jumps in
plunk!

Basho

furu   *ike*   *ya*
old   pond   —

kawazu   *tobikomu*
frog   jump in

mizu   *no*   *oto*
water   [poss.]   sound

on the dead branch
a crow settles—
autumn evening

Basho

kare	*eda*	*ni*	
dead	branch	on	

karasu	*no*	*tomari*	*keri*
crow	[poss.]	settling	[pause]

aki	*no*	*kure*
autumn	[poss.]	evening

48

oblivious
of when it will die,
the cicada chirrs

Basho

yagate	*shinu*
soon	die

keshiki	*wa*	*mie-zu*
indication	as for	appears not

semi	*no*	*koe*
cicada	[poss.]	voice

49

stillness everywhere:
the cicada's voice
pierces rocks

Basho

shizukasa	*ya*	
stillness	[:]	

iwa	*ni*	*shimi-ru*
rocks	into	pierce

semi	*no*	*koe*
cicada	[poss.]	voice

first winter rain:
the monkey too seems to want
a little straw raincoat

Basho

hatsu-shigure
first cold rain

saru	*mo*	*ko-mino wo*
monkey	even	small straw coat

hoshige-nari
seeming to want

I am in Kyo
yet I long for Kyo—
O bird of time!

Basho

Kyō   *nite-mo*
Kyo   though being in

Kyō   natsukashi   ya
Kyo   long for   [—]

hototogisu
cuckoo [bird of time]

there is no one here,
the road is empty.
And evening is falling

Basho

kono   *michi*   *ya*
this   road   [:]

yuku-hito   *nashi*   *ni*
going person   be none   with

aki   *no*   *kure*
autumn   [poss.]   evening

rain frog
riding a banana leaf—
swaying

Kikaku

ama-gaeru
rain frog

bashō	*ni*	*norite*
banana leaf	on	riding

soyogi	*keri*
swinging	*keri*

54

spring sea
all day and all night undulating,
undulating

Buson

haru	*no*	*umi*
spring	[poss.]	sea

hinemosu	*notari*
all day and all night	undulating

notari	*kana*
undulating	kana

the cuckoo flies
until it disappears from view—
out toward the lone island

Basho

hototogisu
cuckoo

kie-yuku   *kata*   *ya*
vanish go   direction   [—]

shima   *hitotsu*
island   one

a sudden shower:
naked I ride
bareback on a horse

Issa

yūdachi   *ya*
sudden shower [:]

hadaka-de   *norishi*
being naked   riding

hadaka   *uma*
naked   horse

summer lightning:
yesterday in the east,
today in the west

Kikaku

inazuma   *ya*
lightning   [:]

kinō   *wa*   *higashi*
yesterday   as for   east

kyō   *wa*   *nishi*
today   as for   west

how admirable,
on seeing lightning,
not to think, "Life too is brief!"

Basho

inazuma	*ni*	
lightning flash	in	
satoranu	*hito*	*no*
enlightened	man	[poss.]
tōtosa	*yo*	
admirableness	[!]	

how nice to take a noonday nap,
feet planted against the wall.
How cool the wall

Basho

| *hiya-hiya* | *to* | |
| cool cool | thus | |

| *kabe* | *wo* | *fumaete* |
| wall | [acc.] | putting foot on |

| *hirune* | *kana* | |
| noon sleep | *kana* | |

60

the end of a short summer's night:
at the edge of town
a shop opens

Buson

| *mijikayo* | *ya* |
| short night | [:] |

| *komise* | *aketaru* |
| small shop | opening |

machihazure
edge of town

the caterpillar's hairs
blow and curl
in the morning breeze

Buson

asakaze	*no*
morning breeze	[subj.]

ke	*wo*	*fukimiyuru*
hair	[acc.]	blow

kemushi	*kana*
hairy caterpillar	*kana*

tart persimmons:
the mother eats the parts
that make the mouth pucker

Issa

shibui	*tako*		
puckery	parts		

haha	*ga*	*kui*	*keri*
mother	[nom.]	eats	[past tense]

yama	*no*	*kaki*	
mountain	[poss.]	persimmons	

keeping a lookout, the mother horse
has her foal
lap up the spring water

Issa

haha-uma   *ga*
mother horse   [nom.]

ban   *shite*   *nomasu*
lookout   does   makes to drink

shimizu   *kana*
spring water   *kana*

breastfeeding her baby
the mother counts
all the flea bites

Issa

nomi	*no*	*ato*
flea	[poss.]	bite marks

kazoe	*nagara*	*ni*
count	while	in

soeji	*kana*
suckle	*kana*

65

I the Toad
appear before you!
I emerge from my thicket!

Issa

makari idetaru   *wa*
appearing before you   as for

kono   *yabu*   *no*
this   thicket   [poss.]

gama   *nite*   *sōrō*
toad   it is   swaggeringly

how did it get all the way over here—
this snail
crawling at my feet?

Issa

ashimoto   *e*
at one's feet   to

itsu   *kitarishi*   *yo*
when   did arrive   [!]

katatsumuri
snail

autumn evening:
soundlessly
a crow passes overhead

Kishu

aki	*no*	*kure*
autumn	[poss.]	evening

karasu	*mo*	*nakade*
crow	even	silent

tōri	*keri*
passes	[past tense]

winter storm:
the peering cat
squints and blinks

Yaso

kogarashi   *ya*
a cold wintry blast   [:]

mabataki   *shigeki*
blinks   keeps on

neko   *no*   *tsura*
cat   [poss.]   face

flea,
whatever you do, *don't jump!* —
in that direction is the *river!*

Issa

tobu	*na*	*nomi*
jump	not	flea

sore	*sore*	*soko*	*wa*
look out	look out	that way	as for

sumidagawa
Sumida River

a butterfly flitters over,
joins a butterfly flittering through the garden—
together they bounce and flutter away

Issa

chō	*ga*	*kite*
butterfly	[nom.]	coming

tsurete	*yuki*	*keri*
in company with	flies off	*keri*

niwa	*no*	*chō*
garden	[poss.]	butterfly

don't kill the fly!—
look—it's *begging* you,
wringing its hands and feet!

Issa

yare utsu na
don't strike

hae	*ga*	*te*	*wo*	*suri*
flies	[nom.]	hands	[acc.]	do

ashi	*wo*	*suru*
feet	[acc.]	do

72

I leave.
You stay.
Two autumns.

Buson

yuku	*ware*	*ni*
going	I	for

todomaru	*nare*	*ni*
staying	you	for

aki	*futatsu*
autumns	two

the dragonfly
alights on the stick
that strikes at it

Kohyo

utsu	*tsue*	*no*
strikes	stick	[poss.]

saki	*ni*	*tomarishi*
tip	on	steps

tombo	*kana*
dragonfly	*kana*

74

the puppy—
because it has no such idea as "autumn has come"—
is naturally enlightened

Issa

aki	kinu	to
autumn	arrived	if

shiranu	koinu	ga
enlightened	puppy	[nom.]

hotoke	kana
Buddha	kana

pissing through my doorway
I make a clean hole
in the snow

Issa

massuguna
straight [as an arrow]

shōben	*ana*	*ya*
piss	a hole	[:]

kado	*no*	*yuki*
door	[poss.]	snow

floating in the winter river
is the carcass of a dead dog
that someone has thrown in

Shiki

fuyukawa   *ni*
winter river   in

sutetaru   *inu*   *no*
thrown away   dog   [poss.]

kabane   *kana*
carcass   *kana*

little sparrow,
get out of the way!
here comes Mr. Horse!

Issa

suzume	*no*	*ko*
sparrow	[poss.]	child

soko noke	*soko noke*
out of the way	out of the way

o-uma	*ga*	*tōru*
Mr. Horse	[nom.]	coming through

killing a few flies,
I gradually get the urge
to slay every last one of them

Seibi

hae	*utte*		
flies	attacking		

tsukusan	*to*	*omou*
become possessed	thus	feel inclined

kokoro	*kana*
mind	kana

only the shell
of the cicada left?
did it sing itself out of existence?

Basho

koe	ni	mina
voice	from	all

nakishimōte	ya
sung away	[:]

semi	no	kara
cicada	[poss.]	shell

even when pursued
a butterfly in its fluttery flight
does not seem especially hurried

Garaku

owarete	*mo*
if pursued	even

isoganu	*furi*	*no*
not hurried	seems	[adjectival phrase]

kochō	*kana*
butterfly	*kana*

deep autumn.
I wonder about my neighbor—
how does he live?

Basho

aki	*fukaki*		
autumn	deepens		

tonari	*wa*	*nani*	*wo*
house next door	as for	what	[acc.]

suru	*hito*	*zo*
do for a living	man	I wonder

alone, I go through a tiny village,
a dark winter day.
A dog barks and barks

Shiki

| *fuyuzare* | | *no* |
| winter dreariness | | [poss.] |

| *komura* | *wo* | *yukeba* |
| village | [acc.] | going through |

| *inu* | *hoyuru* |
| dog | barks |

late fall evening drizzle:
a small boat with a bull on board
crosses the river

Shiki

ushi	tsunde	
bull	on board	

wataru	kobune	ya
crosses over	small boat	[:]

yū-shigure
late autumn evening drizzle

84

snail,
climb Mt. Fuji—
oh slowly

Issa

katatsumuri
snail

sorosoro   *nobore*
slowly slowly   climb

Fuji   *no*   *yama*
Fuji   [poss.]   Mount

85

a large firefly
wavers here, wavers there,
flies away

Issa

ō-hotaru
large firefly

yurari-yurari   *to*
wavers wavers   thus

tōri-keri
passes through [past tense]

86

on the temple bell,
fast asleep—
a butterfly

Buson

tsurigane	*ni*
temple bell	on
tomarite	*nemuru*
settling	sleeps
kochō	*kana*
butterfly	*kana*

on the temple bell
the firefly
gleams

Shiki

tsurigane	*ni*
temple bell	on

tomarite	*hikaru*
settling	gleams

hotaru	*kana*
firefly	kana

a cold rain starting
and me without a hat.
On second thought, who cares?

Basho

kasa	*mo*	*naki*	
hat	even	not	

ware	*wo*	*shigururu*	*ka*
me	[acc.]	get cold rain on	[?]

nanto-nanto
what what

the lost child—
cries sadly, but meanwhile makes grabs
at passing fireflies

Ryusui

mayoi-go   no
lost child   [poss.]

naku   naku   tsukamu
crying   crying   grabs at

hotaru   kana
fireflies   kana

the snake slithers away.
But those eyes that stared at me—
I go on seeing them, still in the grass

Kyoshi

hebi	*nigete*			
snake	fleeing			

ware	*wo*	*mishi*	*me*	*no*
me	[acc.]	had looked at	eyes	[poss.]

kusa	*ni*	*nokoru*
grass	in	remain

whale!
down and down it plunges,
its huge tail soaring higher and higher

Buson

kujira	ochite
whale	going down

iyo-iyo	takaki
more and more	high

o-age	kana
tail up	kana

let the mountain stream
pound the rice for me—
I think I'll take a noonday snooze

Issa

yama-mizu		*ni*	
mountain water		to	
kome	*wo*	*tsukasete*	
rice	[acc.]	causing to hit	
hiru-ne	*kana*		
noon nap	kana		

stirring after a good nap
and with a mouth- and eye-stretching yawn
the cat goes out for a prowl and some lovemaking

Issa

nete	*okite*	
sleeping	getting up	

ō-akubi	*shite*	
great yawn	making	

neko	*no*	*koi*
cat	[poss.]	loving

even a one-foot waterfall
can sound pleasant.
How refreshing the evening cool!

Issa

is-shaku	*no*		
one foot	[poss.]		

taki	*mo*	*oto*	*shite*
waterfall	also	sound	making

yū-suzumi
enjoy the evening cool

95

the skylark school
and the frog school are arguing
over the *proper* way to sing

Shiki

hibari-ha	*to*		
skylark school	and		

kaeru-ha	*to*	*uta*	*no*
frog school	and	song	[poss.]

giron	*kana*		
argument	kana		

butterfly in the garden:
the baby crawls to it, it flies off—
the baby crawls to it again, it flies off—

Issa

niwa	no	chō	ko
garden	[poss.]	butterfly	child

ga	haeba	tobi
[nom.]	when crawls	flies and

haeba	tobu
when crawls	flies and

summer river:
though there is a bridge
my horse prefers to slosh through the water

Shiki

| *natsu-kawa* | *ya* | | |
| summer river | [:] | | |

| *hashi* | *are-do* | | *uma* |
| bridge | though there is | | horse |

| *mizo* | *wo* | *yuku* | |
| water | [acc.] | goes | |

98

the sky and the earth
are obliterated.
The snow steadily falls

Hashin

ten	*mo*	*chi*	*mo*
sky	and	earth	too

nashi	*tada*	*yuki*	*no*
are not	only	snow	[poss.]

furishikiri
falls incessantly

the water pitcher *snap!*ing
in the icy night.
I lie awake listening

Basho

kame		*waruru*	
earthenware jar		sound	
yoru	*no*	*kori*	*no*
night	[poss.]	icy	[poss.]
nezame		*kana*	
waking from sleep		*kana*	

first snow of the year.
The daffodil leaves
bend under the flakes

Basho

hatsuyuki   *ya*
first snow of the season   [—]

suisen   *no*   *ha*   *no*
daffodil   [poss.]   leaf   [poss.]

tawamu   *made*
bending   down

a rough sea—
stretched out immensely, going out toward Sado Isle,
the Milky Way

                              Basho

ara   umi   ya
rough   sea   [—]

sado   ni   yokotau
Sado   toward   extending

ama-no-gawa
heaven's river

THREE HAIKU CITED IN THE TEXT

Matsushima!
Matsushima!
oh! Matsushima!

Basho

matsushima	*ya*
Matsushima	[!]

aa	*matsushima*	*ya*
oh	Matsushima	[!]

matsushima	*ya*
Matsushima	[!]

seven views
were hidden in the mist—
but I heard Mii-dera's bell

Basho

shichi	*kei*	*wa*
seven	views	as for

kiri	*ni*	*kakurete*
mist	in	being hidden

mii	*no*	*kane*
Mii	[poss.]	bell

the world of dew is only a world of dew
and yet—
and yet—

Issa

tsuyu	*no*	*yo*	*wa*
world	of	dew	as for

tsuyu	*no*	*yo*	*nagara*
world	of	dew	yet

sari-nagara
however

Appendix 2

THE LIVES OF FOUR POETS

Basho
(1644–1694)

According to the Japanese, the four greatest haiku poets are Basho, Buson, Issa, and Shiki. Matsuo Basho, one of seven children, was born in Ueno of a father who was a samurai of little distinction and even less means. At an early age Basho was sent to the court of a nobleman as a page and companion of the nobleman's young son, Sengin. The two boys became inseparable friends, and as part of their education, together they studied haiku with a minor poet named Kigin. Sengin died when Basho was 22, and in sorrow over the passing of his close friend, Basho withdrew to a monastery in Kyoto. While there he began a study of calligraphy and Japanese and Chinese classics. Before long he moved to Edo (Tokyo), where, because of his connections and education, he was appointed superintendent of the water works, a sinecure that allowed him to teach haiku writing on the side. After five years of city life, feeling the environment too worldly to satisfy his spiritual needs, he became a devotee of Zen, to which as a monk he applied himself for years. At the age of 40, in a spirit of nonattachment to the things of the world, he began a series of travels by foot that took him far from home for long periods—Daisetz T. Suzuki once called Basho the "poet of Eternal Aloneness"—dying at 50 on one of his wanderings. The two most famous haiku of this first of the great haiku masters are the crow on the dead branch and the frog in the old pond. The crow haiku, which he wrote when he was 35, is usually described as the turning point in haiku writing: it is the first to employ the principle of two contrasting images, each distinct in itself but the two together acquiring significance and a power that go beyond mere imagery. Many consider his old pond haiku, composed when he was 42 and in the full flower of his creativity, the best ever written and the touchstone of all haiku writing, so profound is it in symbolic overtones and so concentrated and pure in its expression.

Taniguchi Buson
(1715–1783)

Very little is known of Buson's life: he was an excellent painter who was quite famed in his time, and his visual bias is apparent in his haiku. Unlike Basho, Buson was eminently worldly, with nothing of the contemplative nature about him. There is in his work no underpinning of Zen or mysticism. Because his haiku are brilliant yet so different from those of Basho, he and Basho are sometimes called "the two pillars of haiku."

Issa
(1763–1827)

To some, much of Issa's work appears sentimental, but to others he is the most "human" and therefore the most loved of all haiku writers. All, however, agree on his genius as a haiku poet. His mother having died when he was around two years old, he was raised by his grandmother, who begged milk to feed him "and never complained of my dirty diapers." The nearly unendurable sadness of his life at the hands of his stepmother (who whipped him "a hundred times a day—a thousand times a month. Tears fell from my eyes 350 days a year") and his subsequent misery over the death of his children cast long shadows over his life. His unhappiness grew so intense that for a time he took to wearing only old and filthy clothing. At the death of his grandmother, when Issa was 13, he went to what is now Tokyo, where, by his early twenties, he was writing haiku under the pen name "Issa," which means "cup of tea." (His real name was Yataro Kobayashi.) Like Basho, he entered a monastic order, but the one he chose was of a worldly and not at all strict sect. He too began a life of travels, which in those earlier centuries were not made as a diversion but as a way of achieving poetic and philosophic discipline—a symbolic pilgrimage, as it were, a way of reaffirming one's values. Not just the physical rigors of travel but the emotional too emphasized that human life, at its core, is lived in individual isolation, that in some profound sense all journeys are only inward. Issa gave beautiful expression to his feelings about existence in his diary, *The Year of My Life*. Written in *haibun,* which is a combination of haiku and a prose that is poetic in its compression, the "year" was an artistic convention: what he described was a composite of many years, a representative segment of his life. And though it is called a travel diary, it is so beautifully laconic and so sparingly simple that it is considered one of the great masterpieces of Japanese literature.

Shiki
(1867–1902)

Possibly the most famous saying of this modern haiku master, in one of many articles he wrote advising beginners on how to write haiku, is "A poem does not mean. A poem makes you feel." Described by those who knew him as "a lover of the truth," Shiki, an ardent devotee of literature, became famous from his early twenties on for his mastery of the haiku form—and notorious for his blasphemous dismissal of four-fifths of Basho's work. No doubt much of Shiki's early iconoclasm (he later changed his mind about Basho's worth) came out of his agnosticism and anticlericalism—and youth. Whatever he did he did with that peculiar passion of those whose life is destined to be short. (He was in the habit of devouring such quantities of persimmons that for reasons of health a doctor finally restricted him to what amounted to a starvation ration of a mere two persimmons a day.) He loved haiku—he was passionate about haiku—he said he could never read enough haiku. He wrote many thousands of them, of which hundreds remain consistently good. But his life was a comet flashing across the sky of Japanese literature. He died at 35, before reaching full artistic maturity. Nevertheless, his understanding of the art of writing was excellent. Some of his advice to haiku poets applies to all forms of creative writing: "Do not write from your head—intellectually—but from your senses. Be natural." "It is best to gather material from everyday experience, not from classic haiku." "Compress. Eliminate every superfluous word." "Study many subjects, become especially familiar with all the arts, but learn to distinguish sharply between what is good and what is bad. Do not, however, write from this knowledge but from your feelings." "Write only for yourself. A haiku must convey feeling to you first. If it does that, it will convey feeling to others also."

Bibliography

Blyth, R. H., *Haiku* (Vols. I–IV). Tokyo: Hoku-seido, 1949.

Henderson, Harold G., *An Introduction to Haiku*. New York: Doubleday Anchor Books, 1958.

Ueda, Makoto, *Matsuo Basho*. New York: Twayne Publishers, Inc., 1970.

Yasuda, Kenneth, *The Japanese Haiku*. Rutland, Vermont, and Tokyo: Charles E. Tuttle Company, 1973.

Yuasa, Nobuyuki, *The Year of My Life* (a translation of Issa's *Oraga Haru*). Berkeley and Los Angeles, University of California Press, 1960.

PRODUCTION CREDITS

Printed and bound for Capra Press by Thomson-Shore, Inc. during April 1979. Typeset by McAdams Type, design and production by Karen Foster. All illustrations by the author.